Body Facts

C O N T E N T S

Collins *Children's Books*
Copyright © HarperCollins Publishers Ltd 1996

Your Body Map

Even if you are doing nothing, your body
is always busy. It is made up of lots of
different organs that work together
to keep you alive and healthy.

Your body's HQ
Your brain allows you to think, and
controls everything that your body
does. Nerves leading from your
brain and spinal cord send out
electrical signals to all parts of
your body and
bring messages
back again. This
is called the
nervous system.

Heart of the matter
Your heart is a muscular pump that
pushes blood around the body all
day and all night. Blood supplies
your body parts with food and oxygen
and removes waste.

A breath of fresh air

Every time you breathe in, air is taken to
your lungs where the oxygen you need is
carried away in the blood. When you
breathe out you get rid of the carbon
dioxide that your body doesn't want.

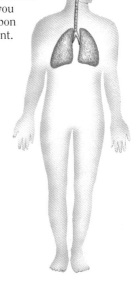

Food on the move

Have you ever wondered what
happens to food between
eating it and going to the toilet?
It travels through a long tube
called your digestive system and on
the way the nutrients you need are
kept while everything else leaves
your body as waste products.

OTHER BITS OF YOUR BODY

You also have eyes for seeing, ears for
hearing, a nose for breathing and smelling
and a tongue for tasting. Your
muscles allow you to move
and your skin holds you together, but without
bones you would look like a blob of jelly.

Bare Bones

There are 206 bones in your body. The longest is the thigh bone, while the smallest – in your middle ear – measures just 3mm. If they weren't all joined together to make a bony frame called the skeleton, they wouldn't be of much use to you.

Broken bones
If you break a bone, doctors use a plaster cast to keep the bone in the right position while the fracture heals.

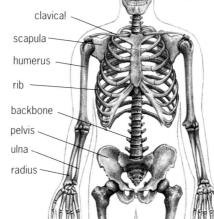

skull

clavical

scapula

humerus

rib

backbone

pelvis

ulna

radius

femur

patella

fibula

tibia

THE BLOOD FACTORY

Bones must be strong and light, so they are hollow, not solid. Each bone is honeycombed with air spaces at either end. The hollow bone shaft is filled with soft marrow. Bone marrow is the body's factory for producing red blood cells and is used for storing fat.

spongy bone

compact bone

bone marrow

4

Jobs for joints

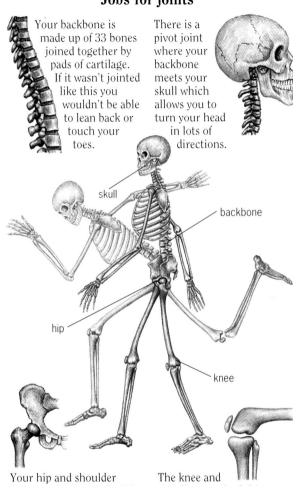

Your backbone is made up of 33 bones joined together by pads of cartilage. If it wasn't jointed like this you wouldn't be able to lean back or touch your toes.

There is a pivot joint where your backbone meets your skull which allows you to turn your head in lots of directions.

skull

backbone

hip

knee

Your hip and shoulder joints are both very flexible because they are ball and socket joints. This kind of joint allows your legs and arms plenty of movement.

The knee and the elbow are both hinge joints and without these you would not be able to sit down, stand up or bend your arms.

Mighty Muscles

Without a skeleton you wouldn't be able to
move, but what moves your skeleton?
Muscles do – about 640 of them are attached
to your bones. The biggest muscle is in
your bottom and the strongest is your
jaw muscle. Muscles are attached to
bones by tough, stringy tendons.

deltoid
lifts arm

pectoralis
pulls arm
toward
body

Pull – don't push
Muscles can pull but they
can't push, so they work in
pairs to move your skeleton.
When one muscle has
pulled a bone in one
direction, its partner has to
pull it back.

When you bend your arm,
your triceps and biceps
muscles are working together.

biceps
bends arm

quadriceps
femoris
straightens
leg

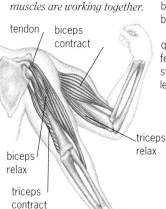

tendon   biceps
contract

triceps
relax

biceps
relax

triceps
contract

6

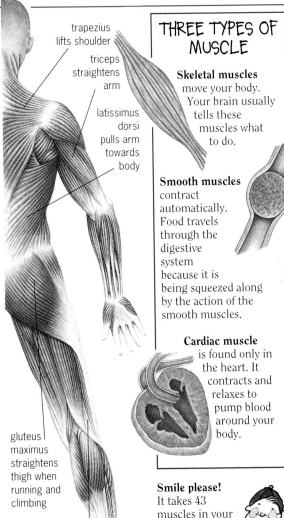

trapezius
lifts shoulder

triceps
straightens
arm

latissimus
dorsi
pulls arm
towards
body

gluteus
maximus
straightens
thigh when
running and
climbing

hamstring
bends knee

THREE TYPES OF MUSCLE

Skeletal muscles move your body. Your brain usually tells these muscles what to do.

Smooth muscles contract automatically. Food travels through the digestive system because it is being squeezed along by the action of the smooth muscles.

Cardiac muscle is found only in the heart. It contracts and relaxes to pump blood around your body.

Smile please!
It takes 43 muscles in your face to frown but only 17 to smile.

What Makes You Grow?

Your life started when one sperm cell met one egg cell and they joined together. This new cell split in half to make two cells and these both then split into two to make four, then eight... and now you probably have over 100 million million cells.

CELL DIVISION...1

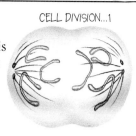

...2

DNA STRAND

DNA
Cells are your body's building blocks. Inside each cell there is a special chemical code called DNA (or deoxyribonucleic acid) which contains all the instructions needed to make and run the cell. Nobody's DNA is the same.

AND 3

CELLS

Cells come in lots of different shapes and sizes and they don't have to be squidgy – just think of bone cells.

Both these cells will now divide again...

5 WEEKS

After a few days you were a bundle of cells, constantly dividing.

You were 8mm long with eyes and a beating heart.

8 WEEKS

You were 3cm long and had arms, legs, fingers and toes.

Divide and multiply

5 MONTHS

You were about 16cm long and started to move about.

7 MONTHS
Your lungs developed.

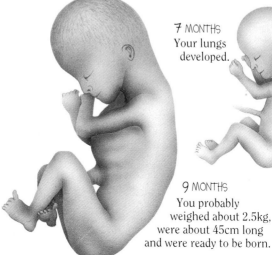

9 MONTHS

You probably weighed about 2.5kg, were about 45cm long and were ready to be born.

Brain Waves

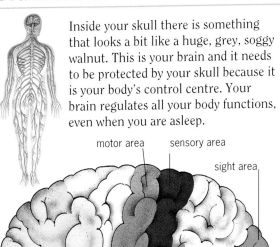

Inside your skull there is something that looks a bit like a huge, grey, soggy walnut. This is your brain and it needs to be protected by your skull because it is your body's control centre. Your brain regulates all your body functions, even when you are asleep.

motor area   sensory area

sight area

thinking area

hearing area

KEY TO THE BRAIN

You use the front part of your brain for thinking and learning. It is also the area that controls your emotions and personality.

The sensory area receives messages from nerves in your skin and allows you to touch and feel.

Messages from the motor area are carried by nerves to your muscles, so that you can move and balance.

Electrical messages from your eyes travel at 400kmh along the optic nerve to the sight area. This part of your brain turns the messages into pictures.

With your hearing area you can make sense of all the sounds picked up by your ears.

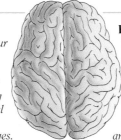

Left brain
The left side of your brain is good at logical thinking. You use your left brain for working out mathematical problems and learning languages.

Right brain
The right side of your brain is good at creative thinking. You use the right side of your brain for appreciating art and music.

ACTUAL FACE

RIGHT SIDE AND ITS MIRROR IMAGE

LEFT SIDE AND ITS MIRROR IMAGE

The human face is not perfectly symmetrical. The right side of your brain controls the left side of your body and vice versa. In the photo sequence above we have cut the actual face in half and matched two right sides and two left sides. You can see how our brain affects the way we look.

Reflex reaction
If you tread on a drawing pin, signals rush along a nerve from your foot to your spinal cord. Before your brain registers the pain a message from the spinal cord to your leg muscle has lifted your foot.

BRAIN BOX

NEURON

There are over 10 thousand million neurons (or nerve cells) in your brain.
Each neuron has tiny branches and may be connected with as many as 25,000 other neurons.

11

Healthy Heart

Your heart is a pump that sends blood all round the body through a network of arteries, veins and capillaries so that every cell is continually supplied with the food and oxygen it needs.

aorta

femoral artery

femoral vein

Blood makes a full circuit of your body in just under a minute.

What is an artery?
Arteries are tubes which carry blood away from the heart. They have thick walls made of muscle. The biggest artery in your body is called the aorta and is as wide as your thumb.

What is a vein?
Veins bring used blood back to the heart so it can be sent to the lungs to pick up more oxygen before going round the body again.

Tiny tubes
Capillaries branch off from every artery and vein, they are the smallest blood vessels in your body and blood cells have to travel through them in single file.

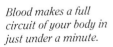

DID YOU KNOW?
If all your arteries, veins and capillaries were joined together end to end they would stretch over 100,000km or two and a half times round the Earth.

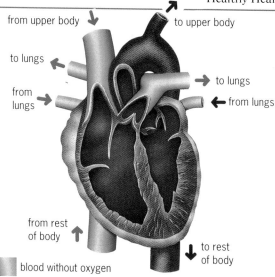

from upper body ↓

to upper body ↑

to lungs ←

to lungs →

from lungs →

← from lungs

from rest of body ↑

to rest of body ↓

▨ blood without oxygen

■ blood with oxygen

Heart test

Your heart contracts more than 60 times a minute. It is about the same size as your fist. Just try clenching your fist every second and see how quickly your hand gets tired!

Finger on the pulse

Your pulse tells you how fast your heart is beating. The easiest place to count your pulse rate is on your wrist.

BLOOD

Blood is made up of cells and a special watery liquid called plasma.

Red blood cells carry oxygen.

White blood cells fight against infections.

Sticky platelets help seal up a wound if you cut yourself.

13

Air Conditioning

Every time you breathe in – about 15 times a minute – air is sucked in through your mouth and nose. It then travels down your trachea to the lungs.

trachea

Cilia are microscopic hairs lining your trachea, they are always moving to waft any dirt trapped in mucus away from your lungs.

Gas swap shop
Your lungs are full of branching passages which fill up with air like a sponge soaking up water. The airways are covered in tiny blood vessels. Oxygen that your body needs enters the blood while unwanted carbon dioxide leaves the blood, ready for breathing out.

lung

Large lungs
If all the passages in your lungs were laid out flat they would cover a tennis court.

Breathing in...
A special sheet of muscle under your lungs, called the diaphragm, pulls down to make more room for them to fill up with air.

...and out
The diaphragm relaxes, so air is squeezed out of your lungs.

diaphragm

Hiccups
Sometimes your diaphragm contracts violently and air is sucked in very fast. When this happens your vocal cords also snap shut, making an odd sound.

Lungs under attack
People with asthma find it difficult to breathe because the airways in their lungs become narrow. They have to inhale special medicines to widen the air passages. Asthma attacks can be triggered by allergies to pollen, dust, animal fur or certain foods.

MAGNIFIED POLLEN GRAINS

NOT TO BE SNEEZED AT

The air we breathe can be dirty, dusty or smoky. If particles irritate your nose, sneezing will get rid of them. The particles are mixed with slimy mucus and are discharged from your mouth at a speed of 160kmh!

Food Processing

You eat when you feel hungry. Food is
your body's fuel. It turns into energy
to keep you alive and healthy.

Where does your food go?
As it passes through the long tube called your
digestive system, the food you have eaten is broken
down so your body can use the parts it needs.

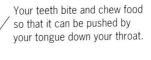

Your teeth bite and chew food
so that it can be pushed by
your tongue down your throat.

Food travels to your stomach
where it is churned around
and mixed with digestive
juices for about four hours.

When this nutritious 'soup'
leaves your stomach, it is
pushed along the small
intestine which is a narrow
coiled tube about 4m long.
Nutrients from the liquid
food are absorbed into
the bloodstream and
taken to the liver.

Busy liver
The liver is your body's processing plant. Blood brings digested food straight to the liver, so that any harmful bacteria or poisons can be removed. Because the liver is such a large, busy organ (doing more than 500 different jobs) it makes lots of heat and helps to keep your body at the right temperature.

Did you know?
Healthy bodies should be made up of about 60 per cent water.

Kidney duo
You have two kidneys which clean the blood to remove unwanted chemicals and make sure that it contains the right amount of salt and water. The waste products and water drain from the kidneys into the bladder, which empties when it gets full.

Monsieur Mangetout
Michel Lotito from France has a most unusual diet. Since 1966 he has eaten...

X 6

X 2

X 7

X 18

X 15

X 1

X 1

WASTE DISPOSAL
Some things you eat are too tough to be digested so they get mixed with dead cells and water in the large intestine before being pushed out of your body when you go to the toilet. You empty about 50kg of solid body waste down the toilet every year.

Eye to Eye

Your eyes work a bit like a camera that is taking pictures all the time.

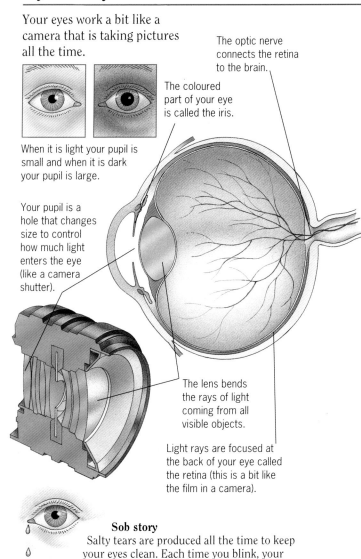

When it is light your pupil is small and when it is dark your pupil is large.

Your pupil is a hole that changes size to control how much light enters the eye (like a camera shutter).

The optic nerve connects the retina to the brain.

The coloured part of your eye is called the iris.

The lens bends the rays of light coming from all visible objects.

Light rays are focused at the back of your eye called the retina (this is a bit like the film in a camera).

Sob story

Salty tears are produced all the time to keep your eyes clean. Each time you blink, your eyelids close and spread the tear fluid over your eyes. You blink about 15 times a minute.

Does this picture show a vase or two faces?

Hold this page up and then hold a glass of water about 12cm in front. What happens to the arrow?

Seeing is believing

Sometimes your brain gets confused by all the information carried from the eyes by the optic nerve. That's why these pictures may not be quite what they seem at first glance.

Which line is longer? Measure them both to find out.

Colour puzzle

Some people are 'colour blind': they cannot tell the difference between certain colours, usually red and green. The girl in this picture is looking at a special pattern to find out if she is colour blind.

DO CARROTS HELP YOU SEE IN THE DARK?

The retina is covered by special light-sensitive cells called rods and cones. You have about six million cone cells and 120 million rod cells in each eye. Rod cells help you see in dim light and they need lots of vitamin A to work properly. One of the best ways of getting enough vitamin A is to eat plenty of carrots!

Hear, Hear!

Although you cannot see them, there are sound waves travelling through the air all around you – like the ripples a stone makes when you throw it into a pond.

1 Our ears are shaped like funnels to catch as many sounds as possible.

2 Sound waves travel down the auditory canal.

Hearing test
You need two ears to help you tell what direction sounds are coming from.

But if a sound comes from directly in front of you or directly behind you it will reach both your ears at exactly the same time. So if you put on a blindfold, you won't be able to tell if someone is clapping in front of you or behind you.

ALL EARS

Bats make very high-pitched squeaks and use the echoes that bounce back to find their way in the dark.

Some animals, like rabbits, can lift up and turn their ears which helps them work out where sounds are coming from.

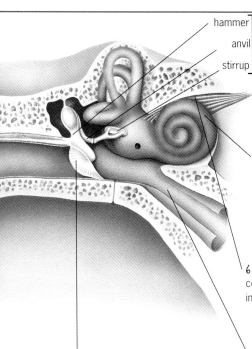

hammer
anvil
stirrup

4 These are the three smallest bones in your body: vibrations from the eardrum travel along this chain of bones to the cochlea.

5 The cochlea is a coiled tube filled with liquid which ripples as the stirrup bone wobbles.

6 Vibrations from the cochlea send nerve impulses to the brain.

3 Sound waves hit a thin piece of skin called the eardrum. The sound waves make the eardrum vibrate just like a real drum being hit.

Your middle ear is connected to the top of your nose by the Eustachian tube.

BALANCING ACT

You use your ears for balance as well as hearing. Tubes inside your ears, called the semi-circular canals, help you balance. They are full of liquid which swirls as your head moves. This tells your brain what position you are in.

SEMI-CIRCULAR
CANALS

21

Smelling and Tasting

It's not a coincidence that your nose is just above your mouth, they need to be close together to make your favourite food even tastier.

Try this!
To find out how important your nose is for tasting, wear a blindfold, hold your nose and take sips from different flavoured drinks. Can you tell which one is which?

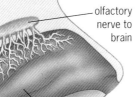

olfactory nerve to brain

nasal cavity

Inside story
Inside your nose there are 25 million smell receptors called olfactory cells. They turn chemical messages into nerve impulses which are then sent to the brain. Your brain is very good at remembering smells and linking them to other memories. The smell of boiled cabbage usually reminds people of school dinners!

SMELLY FACTS
• Humans can distinguish 10,000 different odours, but our sense of smell is not as good as that of the male emperor moth. It can catch the whiff of a female mate 11km away.

• The nastiest smell in the world is produced by the chemical, selenomer captan. It is like a mixture of rotting cabbage, garlic, onions and sewer gas.

• Salmon have an excellent memory for smells. They can find their way back to the river where they were born by recognising its smell even after 18 months at sea.

Map of the tongue

This is a map of the tongue. It shows how it is divided into areas which are used for tasting sweet, salty, sour and bitter foods. If you use small amounts of sugar, salt, lemon juice and strong black coffee you can find the different taste areas on your tongue.

bitter

sour

salty

sweet

DID YOU KNOW?

The durian fruit, which grows in parts of Malaysia, smells disgusting (like rotting meat) but its taste can be addictive.

DURIAN FRUIT

Taste buds

If you look at your tongue you can see that it is covered in little bumps. Between these bumps there are about 10,000 microscopic taste buds. These work as chemical detectors and send nerve signals to the brain's sensory area.

What makes your mouth water?

Saliva is made by glands in your mouth. It mixes with the food you eat to make it easier to swallow. The smell of your favourite food makes your mouth water because the brain sends signals which activate your salivary glands.

It smells like dinner time

Skin Deep

Skin is a waterproof covering that protects your body from harmful germs and stops everything leaking out. But if you could look underneath you'd see a lot more going on.

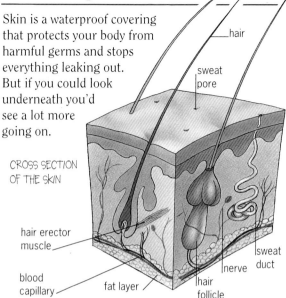

hair

sweat pore

CROSS SECTION OF THE SKIN

hair erector muscle

blood capillary

fat layer

hair follicle

nerve

sweat duct

You need nerves under your skin to feel...

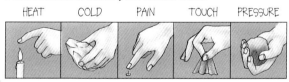

HEAT COLD PAIN TOUCH PRESSURE

HOT WATER

LUKE WARM WATER

COLD WATER

Confusing your nerves
Try this experiment by putting your left index finger in hot water and your right index finger in cold water. Then put them both in luke warm water. What happens?

A BURNING ISSUE

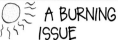

If you have pale skin you are more likely to get burnt if you sit in the sun for too long. People who live in hot countries protect their skin by covering up in cool cotton clothes.

Sweating...

Sweating cools you down because water evaporates from the surface of your skin. You can lose 1 litre of sweat a day in hot weather.

...and shivering

When you shiver the muscles under your skin become active and produce heat to make you feel warmer.

Fingerprints

Everybody has a unique pattern on their fingertips which is why fingerprints can be used by the police to help identify suspects.

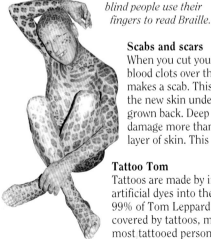

Fingertips are very sensitive – that's why blind people use their fingers to read Braille.

TOM LEPPARD

Scabs and scars

When you cut yourself the blood clots over the wound and makes a scab. This falls off when the new skin underneath has grown back. Deep cuts can damage more than just the top layer of skin. This leaves scars.

Tattoo Tom

Tattoos are made by injecting artificial dyes into the skin. Over 99% of Tom Leppard's body is covered by tattoos, making him the most tattooed person in the world.

Hair, Nails and Teeth

Why is having your nails or your hair cut a painless experience? The bits you cut are actually dead cells.

root

bone

nail bed

dead cells

Did you know?
The keratin your nails are made of also forms the horns, hooves, beaks, fur, feathers and scales of animals.

THE LONGEST NAILS
The five nails on the left hand of Shridar Chillal of Pune, India measured over 4.5 metres in total. The longest of the five was the thumbnail, at over 1 metre.

Keep your hair on
Did you know that the hair you actually see is dead? The living part of your hair comes from a root under the skin. Your body is covered with hairs except for your lips, the soles of your feet and the palms of your hands.

MAGNIFIED HAIRS ON THE SCALP

Open wide

Your 'milk' teeth fall out by age twelve, and they are replaced by permanent teeth. *Incisors* are flat to chop your food up. *Canines* are pointed to grip and tear. *Molars* and *premolars* are broad and flat to crush and grind.

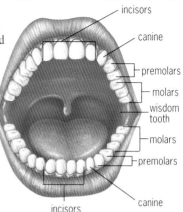

incisors
canine
premolars
molars
wisdom tooth
molars
premolars
canine
incisors

enamel
pulp cavity
gum
dentine
incisors

Tough teeth

Teeth are even harder than your bones. The hardest part of each tooth is the enamel coating. The centre of the tooth is soft and contains nerves and capillaries.

First false teeth?

Evidence of the use of false teeth has been found in Etruscan tombs in Italy dating from 700BC!

HAIR-RAISING FACTS!!!

• The hair of Mata Jagdamba, from India, is 6.4m long.
• Your body has 5 million hairs, of which 100,000 are on your head. You lose 50–100 hairs per day.

• Barbers count on your hair growing 12–15cm per year.
• Can your hair stand on end? Yes, it can, but not obviously, like a cat's. You get goose-bumps when your body hairs stand on end.

Staying Healthy

Your body works hard to keep you healthy,
but you need to look after it too.

Daily diet

A balanced diet is very important for your body.

Rice, potatoes, and pasta contain lots of carbohydrate which gives you energy.

PASTA

About 10% of your body is made of protein and you need to renew it by eating foods which are rich in protein like eggs, beans, fish, nuts and meat.

EGGS

Fat is stored in the body as a reserve of energy and also to keep you warm. Olive oil, butter and cheese are all kinds of fats.

CHEESE

Your body also needs small amounts of about 20 different minerals. Dark green vegetables contain iron which is used to make red blood cells, and milk is rich in calcium which strengthens bones and teeth.

MILK

VEGETABLES

Most of the 15 different vitamins which keep you healthy are found in fruit and vegetables. They are also added to breakfast cereals. Vitamin D is made by the skin when it is exposed to sunlight.

CEREAL

Fibre is not digested but makes the muscles in your intestines work properly. High-fibre foods include wholemeal bread and vegetables.

BREAD

Exercise is good for you!
When you exercise you use lots of different muscles and joints in your body. This keeps them working properly. Exercise also makes your heart stronger and your breathing more efficient.

	A	B	C
CYCLING	★★★	★	★★
FOOTBALL	★★	★★	★★
SWIMMING	★★★	★★★	★★★
JOGGING	★★★	★	★
WALKING	★		
TENNIS	★	★★	★
GYMNASTICS	★	★★★	
SQUASH	★★	★★	

A STAMINA B SUPPLENESS
C STRENGTH

BODY HAZARDS

Tobacco smoke contains thousands of different chemicals, many of which can damage the lungs.

People who drink too much alcohol suffer from kidney and liver failure, stomach ulcers, and even brain damage.

Stress is not good for your body. You should try to stay relaxed by taking exercise and getting enough sleep.

Sweet dreams
Sleep gives the body a chance to relax and repair itself. You only grow while you are asleep. You dream because your brain is very active during the night, sorting out information that it has received.

Good night, I've got some growing to do!

Vital Statistics

Some people have record-breaking bodies but whoever you are, your body is just amazing.

Baby boom
A woman living in 18th-century Russia gave birth to 69 children over a period of about 40 years.

Muscle man
In 1921 Herman Gomer of Germany lifted 24 men sitting on a plank. The plank was balanced on the soles of his feet!

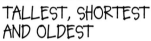

TALLEST, SHORTEST AND OLDEST

• Robert Wadlow was the tallest man ever recorded. When he was 5 years old he was already 1.63m tall and he reached a height of 2.72m by the time he died in 1940 at the age of 22.
• The shortest person on record was Pauline Musters from Holland. When she died at the age of 19 in 1895, she measured just 61cm.

• Jeanne Louise Calment from France is the oldest living person. She was born on 21 February 1875.

YOUR EYE MUSCLES MOVE 100,000 TIMES A DAY

Did you know?

Your body is made up of:

 enough iron to make a nail

 enough calcium to make a tin of paint

 enough fat to make seven bars of soap

enough muscle to make a hundred burgers.

Nerve signals travel at 450kmh.

The longest nerve in your body – the sciatic nerve – can be up to one metre long.

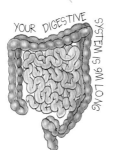

YOUR DIGESTIVE SYSTEM IS 9M LONG

LAID FLAT, YOUR SKIN WOULD COVER A SINGLE BED

CELL RECORDS

• You make about 300 million new red blood cells in a minute.

• 5,000 human cells are about the size of a grain of sand.

• Cells lining your intestines get worn away after about three days. Bone cells live for up to 30 years, and some brain cells last a lifetime.

31

First published in 1996 by HarperCollins Children's Books,
A Division of HarperCollins Publishers Ltd,
77-85 Fulham Palace Road,
London W6 8JB
ISBN: 0 00 197907 8

Illustrations by Siena Artworks, London
Cartoons by Charlotte Hard

Photographs: Frank Spooner Pictures/ Gamma /Santash Basak 26l; Jo Lomax /Wildcat Collection 25b; Range /Bettmann 30r; Rex Features /Sipa Press /Tschaen 30l; Science Photo Library /Prof. Motta, Correr & Nottola, University 'La Sapienza', Rome 14, /Dr Jeremy Burgess 15, /Adam Hart-Davis 19, /Martin Dohrn 23, /Will & Deni McIntyre 25c, /David Scharf 26r.

All rights reserved. No part of this publication may be reproduced, stored in a retrieval system, or transmitted, in any form or by any means, electronic, mechanical, photocopying or otherwise, without the permission of HarperCollins Publishers Ltd

A CIP record for this book is available from the British Library

Printed and bound in Hong Kong